D1706812

Chapter 1: Introduction to Computer Hardware Repair and Maintenance

Importance of Computer Hardware Maintenance

In today's technology-driven world, computer hardware has become an integral part of our daily lives, powering everything from personal computers to smartphones and servers. Understanding the importance of computer hardware maintenance is crucial for ensuring optimal performance, prolonging the lifespan of your devices, and preventing potential issues that may disrupt your workflow.

Regular hardware maintenance helps in the early detection of potential problems, allowing for timely repairs or replacements. By identifying and addressing hardware issues before they escalate, you can avoid costly repairs and minimize downtime. Neglecting maintenance can lead to overheating, component failures, data loss, and decreased overall performance.

Hardware maintenance also plays a significant role in preserving the longevity of your devices. Proper cleaning, dust removal, and cooling system maintenance prevent the accumulation of debris and ensure optimal airflow, reducing the risk of overheating. Additionally, regular maintenance routines such as updating firmware and drivers help keep your hardware up to date and compatible with the latest software and security patches.

Moreover, hardware maintenance contributes to the stability and reliability of your computer system. Well-maintained hardware components result in smoother operation, faster response times, and fewer unexpected crashes or system failures. This is particularly important for professionals and businesses relying on their computer systems for critical tasks, as any disruption can lead to significant productivity losses.

By dedicating time and effort to hardware maintenance, you take control of your computing experience. You can enjoy a more efficient and reliable system, safeguard your valuable data, and maximize the lifespan of your hardware investment. In the following chapters, we will explore various maintenance techniques, troubleshooting methods, and best practices to empower you with the knowledge and skills needed to keep your computer hardware in optimal condition.

Basic Tools for Hardware Repair

When it comes to computer hardware repair, having the right tools at your disposal is essential. These tools not only enable you to diagnose and fix hardware issues but also ensure that repairs are conducted safely and efficiently. In this section, we will explore some of the basic tools that every aspiring hardware technician or DIY enthusiast should have in their toolkit.

Screwdriver Set: A set of precision screwdrivers is indispensable for working with computer hardware. Different types and sizes of screws are used in various components, such as the CPU, hard drive, and motherboard. Having a variety of screwdrivers with interchangeable heads ensures that you have the right tool for the job.

Anti-Static Wrist Strap: Static electricity can cause irreparable damage to sensitive electronic components. An anti-static wrist strap, connected to a grounded surface, helps discharge static electricity from your body and prevents it from damaging computer parts during repairs or upgrades.

Needle-nose Pliers: These slim and long-nosed pliers come in handy for reaching into tight spaces and gripping small components or cables. They are useful for removing or installing jumpers, connectors, or small screws.

Thermal Paste and Isopropyl Alcohol: Thermal paste is used to improve the transfer of heat between the CPU and its heatsink. Isopropyl alcohol is used to clean the old thermal paste before applying a fresh layer. These substances ensure optimal cooling performance and prevent overheating.

Cable Ties and Velcro Straps: Keeping cables organized inside your computer case enhances airflow and reduces clutter. Cable ties or Velcro straps help secure and manage cables, preventing them from blocking fans or obstructing other components.

Diagnostic Software and USB Drive: Diagnostic software tools, such as hardware diagnostic programs and bootable USB drives, are invaluable for troubleshooting hardware issues. These tools allow you to perform tests, monitor system health, and diagnose problems without disassembling the entire computer.

Remember, these are just a few examples of the basic tools needed for hardware repair. Depending on the complexity of the repairs or upgrades you plan to undertake, you may need additional specialized tools such as a multimeter, wire cutters/strippers, or a heat gun.

Safety Measures and Precautions

When working with computer hardware, it is crucial to prioritize safety to protect both yourself and the components you are handling. This section highlights some important safety measures and precautions to follow during hardware repair and maintenance.

Power Off and Unplug: Before opening the computer case or performing any hardware repairs, always ensure that the device is powered off and unplugged. This prevents the risk of electric shock and safeguards against accidental power surges or short circuits.

Ground Yourself: Static electricity can damage sensitive electronic components. To prevent static discharge, use an anti-static wrist strap connected to a grounded surface or touch a grounded object before handling any hardware components. This helps dissipate static electricity from your body.

Use Proper Handling Techniques: Handle hardware components with care. Avoid touching sensitive parts, such as gold-plated connectors or pins, to prevent damage from oils and residues on your hands. Hold components by their edges or designated non-sensitive areas.

Avoid ESD-Sensitive Areas: Electrostatic discharge (ESD) can cause irreversible damage to electronic components. Avoid working on ESD-sensitive areas, such as carpets, and use anti-static mats or work on surfaces that dissipate static electricity.

Maintain a Clean Workspace: Keep your workspace organized and clutter-free. Remove any unnecessary objects or liquids that could potentially damage or interfere with the hardware. Additionally, clean the work area regularly to prevent dust or debris from entering the components.

Follow Manufacturer Instructions: Always refer to the manufacturer's documentation and instructions for hardware repairs or upgrades. Each component may have specific handling requirements or installation procedures that need to be followed for proper functioning and warranty compliance.

Beware of Sharp Edges and Moving Parts: Some computer hardware components may have sharp edges or moving parts, such as cooling fans.

Take caution when handling these components to avoid injury. Use appropriate tools or wear protective gloves if necessary.

Keep Track of Screws and Small Parts: During disassembly, keep track of screws and small parts by using magnetic trays or labeling them. This ensures that you can reassemble the hardware correctly and prevents the risk of losing or misplacing important components.

Stay Updated and Educated: Hardware technology evolves rapidly, and new safety considerations may arise. Stay updated on best practices and safety guidelines by referring to reputable sources, attending workshops or training sessions, and keeping informed about industry standards and recommendations.

Chapter 2: Understanding Computer Components

Central Processing Unit (CPU)

The Central Processing Unit, or CPU, is often referred to as the "brain" of a computer. It is a critical component responsible for executing instructions and performing calculations. Understanding the CPU and its role in computer systems is fundamental to gaining insight into the overall functionality and performance of a computer. In this section, we will explore the key aspects of the CPU and its significance in the world of computer hardware.

The CPU is responsible for executing instructions and coordinating various tasks within a computer system. It performs calculations, manages data transfer between different components, and controls the overall operation of the system. The CPU contains an arithmetic logic unit (ALU) for mathematical calculations and logical operations, as well as a control unit that manages the execution of instructions.

CPUs are designed based on specific architectures, such as x86, ARM, or PowerPC. Each architecture defines the instruction set and organization of the CPU, influencing its performance, power efficiency, and compatibility with software applications. It is essential to consider the CPU architecture when selecting or upgrading a computer system, as it determines software compatibility and overall performance.

The clock speed of a CPU refers to the number of instructions it can execute per second. It is measured in gigahertz (GHz). A higher clock speed generally indicates faster processing capabilities. Additionally, CPUs can have multiple cores, which enable them to handle multiple tasks simultaneously. More cores generally result in better multitasking performance and improved overall system performance.

CPUs have built-in cache memory that stores frequently accessed data and instructions, allowing for faster access compared to accessing data from the main memory (RAM). The cache memory consists of multiple levels, with each level having different capacities and speeds. Larger cache sizes and higher cache speeds contribute to improved CPU performance.

TDP is a measure of the amount of heat a CPU generates under normal operating conditions. It is an important consideration for system builders and enthusiasts, as it affects cooling requirements and overall system power consumption. CPUs with higher TDP values generally require more robust cooling solutions to prevent overheating.

Understanding CPU compatibility with the motherboard and socket is crucial when considering upgrades. Different CPUs have specific socket requirements, and it is essential to ensure compatibility to avoid compatibility issues and potential damage to the hardware.

Random Access Memory (RAM)

Random Access Memory, commonly known as RAM, is a crucial component of a computer system that plays a vital role in its performance and functionality. Understanding RAM and its characteristics is essential for optimizing system performance and ensuring smooth operation. In this section, we will explore the key aspects of RAM and its significance in computer hardware.

RAM serves as the primary temporary storage for data and instructions that the CPU needs to access quickly. It provides the working space for actively running programs and processes, enabling fast data retrieval and execution. RAM allows for efficient multitasking and influences overall system performance.

RAM is available in various capacities, typically measured in gigabytes (GB) or terabytes (TB). The capacity determines the amount of data that can be stored and accessed simultaneously. Additionally, RAM has different speeds, measured in megahertz (MHz) or gigahertz (GHz). Higher RAM speeds allow for faster data transfer between the CPU and RAM, enhancing overall system responsiveness.

Some motherboards support dual-channel or multi-channel memory configurations, which utilize multiple memory modules simultaneously. This setup can improve memory bandwidth and performance by allowing data to be accessed in parallel. Understanding the memory configuration capabilities of your motherboard can help maximize RAM performance.

CAS (Column Address Strobe) latency refers to the delay between the CPU's request for data and the availability of the requested data from RAM. It is measured in clock cycles. Lower CAS latency indicates faster response times and better RAM performance. RAM modules also have other timing parameters that affect their performance, such as RAS (Row Address Strobe) and tRCD (Row-to-Column Delay).

Upgrading RAM can be an effective way to enhance system performance. When considering a RAM upgrade, it is important to ensure compatibility with the motherboard and the existing RAM modules. Factors such as the type (DDR3, DDR4, etc.), speed, and capacity should be taken into account to ensure proper installation and optimal performance.

Proper RAM management involves optimizing the allocation of memory resources to running applications and processes. This includes closing unnecessary programs, monitoring resource usage, and configuring virtual memory settings. Effective RAM management can prevent system slowdowns caused by insufficient memory availability.

Storage Devices

Storage devices are integral components of a computer system that are responsible for long-term data storage. Understanding the different types of storage devices, their characteristics, and their role in data management is crucial for effectively utilizing computer hardware. In this section, we will explore the key aspects of storage devices and their significance in the world of computer hardware.

Hard Disk Drives (HDDs): Hard disk drives are traditional storage devices that use rotating magnetic disks to store data. They provide large storage capacities at affordable prices, making them suitable for storing vast amounts of data. HDDs are commonly used for general-purpose storage and are available in various capacities, typically measured in terabytes (TB).

Solid-State Drives (SSDs): Solid-state drives are a newer storage technology that use flash memory chips to store data. SSDs offer faster data access and transfer speeds, improved reliability, and better shock resistance compared to HDDs. They are particularly advantageous for applications that require fast read and write speeds, such as operating system installations and software loading.

NVMe Drives: NVMe (Non-Volatile Memory Express) drives are a type of SSD that leverages a high-speed interface and protocol designed specifically for flash storage. NVMe drives offer even faster data transfer speeds and reduced latency compared to traditional SSDs, resulting in improved system responsiveness. They are often used in high-performance computing environments or as boot drives for operating systems.

External Storage Devices: External storage devices provide additional storage capacity that can be easily connected to a computer system via USB,

Thunderbolt, or other interfaces. External hard drives and SSDs offer portability and flexibility, allowing users to back up data, expand storage capacity, or transfer files between devices conveniently.

Optical Drives: Optical drives, such as CD/DVD drives and Blu-ray drives, use lasers to read and write data on optical discs. While their usage has declined with the rise of digital media, they are still utilized for tasks like installing software, playing media, or creating backups. However, many modern computers no longer include built-in optical drives.

Cloud Storage: Cloud storage services allow users to store and access their data over the internet. This type of storage offers the advantage of remote accessibility, data synchronization across devices, and the ability to easily share files with others. Cloud storage can be used as a complement to local storage devices for backup purposes or as a primary storage solution.

Graphics Processing Unit (GPU)

The Graphics Processing Unit, or GPU, is a specialized component responsible for rendering images, videos, and graphics-intensive tasks on a computer system. GPUs play a critical role in gaming, multimedia production, and other visually demanding applications. Understanding the GPU and its significance in computer hardware is essential for maximizing graphics performance and overall user experience. In this section, we will explore the key aspects of GPUs and their role in modern computing.

The primary function of a GPU is to render graphics and images by performing complex calculations and rendering techniques. GPUs excel at parallel processing, allowing them to handle numerous calculations simultaneously. This parallel processing power is particularly beneficial for tasks such as 3D rendering, video editing, and computer-aided design (CAD).

GPUs can be either dedicated or integrated. Dedicated GPUs are separate components with their own memory and processing units, designed specifically for graphics-intensive tasks. They offer higher performance and are commonly found in gaming computers and workstations. Integrated GPUs, on the other hand, are built into the computer's central processing unit (CPU) and share system memory. Integrated GPUs are more suitable for general-purpose computing and less demanding graphics tasks.

CUDA (Compute Unified Device Architecture) and OpenCL (Open Computing Language) are programming frameworks that enable developers to harness the computational power of GPUs for non-graphics tasks. These frameworks allow GPUs to be utilized for general-purpose computing, such as scientific simulations, machine learning, and data processing. Leveraging the parallel processing capabilities of GPUs can significantly accelerate these types of applications.

GPUs have their own dedicated memory called Video RAM (VRAM), which is used to store graphical data and textures. The amount of VRAM determines how much graphical data the GPU can handle at once. Higher VRAM capacities are beneficial for running games at higher resolutions and settings. Additionally, memory bandwidth plays a crucial role in GPU performance, as it determines how quickly data can be transferred to and from the VRAM.

GPUs can generate a significant amount of heat during operation, particularly when running demanding graphics applications. Proper cooling solutions, such as fans or liquid cooling systems, are necessary to maintain optimal operating temperatures. Additionally, high-performance GPUs often have higher power requirements and may require additional power connectors from the power supply.

Motherboard

The motherboard is the central component that connects and houses various hardware components within a computer system. It serves as a communication hub, facilitating data transfer between different components such as the CPU, RAM, storage devices, and expansion cards. Understanding the motherboard and its role in computer hardware is essential for troubleshooting, upgrading, and maintaining a functional and efficient system. In this section, we will explore the key aspects of motherboards and their significance in modern computing.

Motherboards come in different form factors, which determine their physical dimensions, layout, and compatibility with computer cases. Common form factors include ATX, Micro-ATX, and Mini-ITX. Choosing the appropriate form factor ensures compatibility with the computer case and determines the number and types of expansion slots available for adding additional components.

The motherboard's CPU socket determines the type and generation of processors it can support. CPUs have specific socket requirements, such as Intel's LGA or AMD's AM4, and it is essential to select a compatible CPU and motherboard combination. Understanding CPU compatibility ensures proper installation and optimal performance.

Motherboards feature expansion slots for adding various expansion cards, such as graphics cards, sound cards, and network adapters. Expansion slots utilize standards like PCI Express (PCIe) and legacy slots like PCI. Understanding the available expansion slots allows for future expansion and customization based on specific needs.

They also provide slots for installing RAM modules, and the number of slots determines the maximum memory capacity the system can support. Different motherboards support specific types of RAM, such as DDR4 or DDR3. Understanding the RAM slots and memory support is crucial when upgrading or adding more memory to the system.

Another thing they offer is different storage interfaces, such as SATA (Serial ATA) and M.2, for connecting storage devices like hard drives and SSDs. Understanding the available storage interfaces and their specifications allows for selecting the appropriate storage devices and maximizing data transfer speeds.

Motherboards provide a range of I/O ports and connectors for connecting peripherals and external devices. These include USB ports, audio jacks,

Ethernet ports, display ports, and more. Understanding the available I/O options ensures compatibility with peripherals and enables the seamless integration of devices into the system.

Power Supply Unit (PSU)

The Power Supply Unit, or PSU, is a critical component that provides electrical power to all the other hardware components in a computer system. It converts the AC (alternating current) power from the wall outlet into the DC (direct current) power required by the computer's internal components. Understanding the PSU and its role in computer hardware is crucial for ensuring stable and reliable power delivery to the system. In this section, we will explore the key aspects of PSUs and their significance in maintaining a properly functioning computer system.

Power Output and Efficiency: PSUs come in various wattages, representing their power output capacity. It is essential to choose a PSU with sufficient power output to meet the requirements of the components in your system. Additionally, PSU efficiency, expressed as a percentage, indicates how effectively it converts AC power to DC power.

Higher-efficiency PSUs generate less heat and waste less energy.

Connectors and Compatibility: PSUs feature different connectors for supplying power to various components. Common connectors include the 24-pin ATX connector for the motherboard, 4-pin or 8-pin connectors for the CPU, and SATA and PCIe connectors for storage drives and expansion cards. Ensuring compatibility between the PSU connectors and the components in your system is crucial for proper installation and functionality.

Modular vs. Non-Modular PSUs: PSUs can be modular or non-modular. Non-modular PSUs come with a fixed set of cables permanently attached to the unit. Modular PSUs, on the other hand, allow you to connect only the necessary cables, reducing cable clutter and improving airflow within the system. Modular PSUs offer greater flexibility for cable management but may be slightly more expensive.

Power Protection and Safety Features: PSUs often incorporate various protection mechanisms to safeguard the system and its components. These include overvoltage protection (OVP), undervoltage protection (UVP), overcurrent protection (OCP), short circuit protection (SCP), and over-temperature protection (OTP). These features help prevent damage to the hardware in the event of power fluctuations or faults.

Cooling and Fan Noise: PSUs generate heat during operation, and proper cooling is essential for maintaining optimal performance and reliability. PSU cooling is typically achieved through built-in fans that expel hot air from the unit. The size and quality of the fan can affect the cooling efficiency and the amount of noise produced. Consideration should be given to selecting a PSU with an adequate cooling solution that balances performance and noise levels.

Chapter 3: Troubleshooting Common Hardware Issues

Identifying and Diagnosing Hardware Problems

Identifying and diagnosing hardware problems is a fundamental skill in computer hardware repair and maintenance. Understanding how to identify and troubleshoot common hardware issues empowers you to efficiently resolve problems and ensure the optimal performance of your computer system. In this section, we will explore the key steps and techniques for identifying and diagnosing hardware problems effectively.

When encountering a hardware issue, start by gathering information about the problem. Note any error messages, unusual behavior, or specific symptoms exhibited by the system. This information will serve as valuable clues during the troubleshooting process.

Perform a visual inspection of the hardware components. Look for any physical damage, loose connections, or signs of overheating such as burn marks or swollen capacitors. Inspecting the cables, connectors, and ports is also crucial to ensure proper connectivity.

Conduct hardware tests to identify faulty components. There are various diagnostic tools and software available for testing hardware components, such as the CPU, RAM, hard drives, and graphics card. Running comprehensive hardware tests can help pinpoint specific hardware issues.

When troubleshooting hardware problems, it is essential to isolate the problematic component. One effective method is to disconnect or remove non-essential hardware components one by one and test the system's functionality after each removal. This process helps identify whether the problem lies with a specific component or a combination of components.

While troubleshooting hardware issues, it's important to consider potential software factors that could contribute to the problem. Conflicts with device drivers, incompatible software, or operating system issues can sometimes manifest as hardware problems. Updating drivers, running malware scans, and performing software updates can help resolve such issues.

Maintain a record of hardware issues encountered and the troubleshooting steps taken. This documentation serves as a reference for future troubleshooting and can assist in identifying recurring issues. Additionally, researching specific hardware problems, error codes, or symptoms online can provide valuable insights and solutions.

By following these steps and techniques for identifying and diagnosing hardware problems, you can effectively troubleshoot and resolve common hardware issues. Developing strong problem-solving skills and being familiar with hardware components and their interactions will enable you to address hardware problems efficiently. In the subsequent sections, we will continue to explore essential troubleshooting techniques and strategies for maintaining a reliable computer system.

Overheating and Cooling Solutions

Overheating is a common hardware issue that can lead to system instability, performance degradation, and even permanent damage to computer components. Understanding the causes of overheating and implementing effective cooling solutions is crucial for maintaining optimal performance and prolonging the lifespan of your hardware. In this section, we will explore the importance of temperature management, common causes of overheating, and various cooling solutions.

Proper temperature management is essential to ensure the reliable operation of computer hardware. Excessive heat can cause components to throttle their performance or even shut down to prevent damage. Maintaining optimal operating temperatures improves system stability, reduces the risk of hardware failures, and extends the lifespan of your components.

Several factors can contribute to overheating in a computer system. Dust accumulation on components, improper airflow within the case, outdated or malfunctioning fans, inadequate thermal paste application on the CPU, and overclocking without proper cooling are common causes. Identifying the underlying cause is crucial for implementing effective cooling solutions.

Regular cleaning and dust removal are essential to prevent overheating. Dust accumulation on fans, heat sinks, and vents restricts airflow, hindering proper cooling. Using compressed air or a vacuum cleaner with appropriate attachments, carefully clean the components to remove dust. Pay close attention to CPU and GPU fans, as well as heat sink fins.

Optimizing airflow within the computer case helps dissipate heat more effectively. Ensure that cables are neatly organized and do not obstruct the airflow path. Installing additional case fans or upgrading to more efficient ones can enhance airflow. Properly positioning intake and exhaust fans to create a balanced airflow pattern is crucial for efficient cooling.

The CPU is a major heat-generating component in a computer system. Ensuring proper thermal management is vital. Apply a thin and even layer of thermal paste between the CPU and heat sink to improve heat transfer. Installing an aftermarket CPU cooler with improved cooling performance can be beneficial, especially for high-performance systems.

Graphics cards (GPUs) are another component prone to overheating, particularly during demanding tasks like gaming or GPU-intensive applications. Ensure that the GPU's fan or heatsink is clean and free from dust. Consider installing additional case fans to provide direct airflow to the GPU. Upgrading to a more efficient GPU cooler or using aftermarket cooling solutions can also help reduce GPU temperatures.

Power and Connectivity Issues

Power and connectivity issues can disrupt the normal functioning of a computer system and hinder productivity. Understanding the common causes of power and connectivity problems, as well as implementing effective solutions, is essential for maintaining a reliable and efficient computer setup. In this section, we will explore the importance of power management, common power-related issues, and connectivity troubleshooting techniques.

Proper power management is crucial for the stable operation of a computer system. Ensure that your system is connected to a reliable power source and use surge protectors or uninterruptible power supply (UPS) units to safeguard against power surges or outages. Avoid overloading power outlets and make sure the power cables and connectors are in good condition.

A faulty or inadequate power supply can cause various power-related issues. Check if the power supply unit (PSU) is properly connected and providing sufficient power to all the components. Test the PSU using a power supply tester or try a different PSU to rule out power supply-related problems.

During the computer's startup, the Power-On Self-Test (POST) checks the hardware for any errors. If the computer fails the POST, it may indicate power-related issues. Check the connections of power cables, RAM modules, and expansion cards. Reseating or replacing these components can help resolve POST errors.

Connectivity issues can arise due to various factors, including faulty cables, network adapters, or incorrect network configurations. Start by checking physical connections, ensuring Ethernet cables are securely plugged in, and Wi-Fi connections are stable. Use diagnostic tools or command line utilities to check network configurations and troubleshoot connectivity problems.

Outdated or incompatible drivers and software can lead to power and connectivity issues. Ensure that all drivers, including those for the motherboard, network adapters, and peripherals, are up to date. Update firmware for network devices, such as routers or modems, to address compatibility issues.

For network-related connectivity problems, perform basic network troubleshooting steps. Restart routers or modems, check network settings, and verify DNS configurations. Use network diagnostic tools to identify and resolve issues such as IP conflicts, incorrect IP configurations, or DNS resolution problems.

Memory and Storage Problems

Memory and storage problems can significantly impact the performance and functionality of a computer system. Identifying and resolving issues related to memory (RAM) and storage devices (hard drives, SSDs) are essential for maintaining optimal system operation. In this section, we will explore common memory and storage problems, as well as effective troubleshooting techniques.

Insufficient Memory (RAM): Insufficient RAM can cause system slowdowns and even lead to crashes. Monitor the memory usage of your system and identify if it frequently reaches or exceeds its maximum capacity. Consider upgrading the RAM to a higher capacity if your system frequently struggles with multitasking or running resource-intensive applications.

Memory Errors and Testing: Memory errors can manifest as system crashes, program failures, or unexpected reboots. Use memory diagnostic tools, such as Memtest86, to test the RAM for errors. Running memory tests can help identify faulty memory modules. If errors are detected, replacing the faulty module is necessary.

Storage Device Failure: Hard drives and solid-state drives (SSDs) can fail over time, leading to data loss and system instability. Look for signs of a failing storage device, such as slow performance, unusual noises, or frequent file corruption. Regularly back up important data to prevent loss in case of a storage device failure. Consider replacing a failing storage device promptly.

Disk Fragmentation: Disk fragmentation occurs when files are scattered across different physical locations on a hard drive, leading to slower read and write speeds. Regularly defragmenting the hard drive can improve overall system performance. Utilize the built-in defragmentation tools in the operating system or consider third-party software for more advanced defragmentation options.

Disk Errors and Scanning: Disk errors can cause system crashes or prevent access to data. Use disk scanning tools, such as CHKDSK (Check Disk) on Windows or fsck on Linux, to check for and repair disk errors. Running regular disk scans can help maintain the health and integrity of your storage devices.

Storage Optimization: Optimize your storage devices to improve performance and efficiency. This includes removing unnecessary files, uninstalling unused applications, and organizing files in a logical manner. Consider utilizing disk cleanup tools or disk management utilities provided by the operating system to free up disk space and improve storage performance.

Display and Graphics Issues

Display and graphics issues can be frustrating, affecting your ability to work, game, or enjoy multimedia content. Troubleshooting and resolving problems related to the display and graphics components are important for maintaining a visually optimal computing experience. In this section, we will explore common display and graphics issues, as well as effective solutions to address them.

No Display or Blank Screen: If you encounter a situation where your monitor shows no display or a blank screen, start by checking the physical connections between your computer and the monitor. Ensure that the cables are securely connected and try reseating them if necessary. If using a desktop computer, verify that the graphics card is properly seated in the motherboard slot. In case of a laptop, try connecting an external monitor to determine if the issue lies with the display or the graphics card.

Resolution and Display Settings: Incorrect resolution or display settings can result in distorted or fuzzy visuals. Adjust the display settings to match the recommended resolution for your monitor. If the text appears too small or large, you can also adjust the font scaling options in the operating system. Additionally, ensure that the refresh rate is set to an appropriate value supported by your monitor.

Graphics Driver Issues: Outdated or incompatible graphics drivers can lead to display problems. Update the graphics drivers to the latest version provided by the manufacturer. You can usually download and install the drivers from the manufacturer's website or use the automatic driver update utility provided by the operating system. If the issue persists, try rolling back to a previous version of the graphics driver to see if that resolves the problem.

Artifacts and Distorted Graphics: Artifacts, such as flickering, pixelation, or strange patterns on the screen, may indicate issues with the graphics card or its drivers. Ensure that the graphics card is properly cooled to prevent overheating, as excessive heat can cause artifacts. If the problem persists, update or reinstall the graphics drivers, and if necessary, test the graphics card in another system to determine if it is the source of the issue.

Multiple Monitor Setup: If you are using multiple monitors and encountering issues, verify that all connections are secure and the cables are not damaged. Check the display settings to ensure that the monitors are properly detected and configured. If one monitor is not displaying anything or showing incorrect visuals, try swapping the connections or using a different cable to isolate the problem.

Graphics-intensive Applications: If you experience graphical issues while running graphics-intensive applications, such as games or 3D modeling software, ensure that your system meets the minimum hardware requirements. Update the graphics drivers to the latest version optimized for the specific application. Adjust the graphics settings within the application to a lower level if your system struggles to handle the demands of the software.

BIOS and Firmware Updates

Keeping the BIOS (Basic Input/Output System) and firmware of your computer up to date is crucial for ensuring system stability, compatibility, and security. In this section, we will explore the importance of BIOS and firmware updates, the risks of outdated firmware, and the steps involved in safely updating them.

The BIOS is a software component embedded in the computer's motherboard, responsible for initializing hardware during the boot process. Firmware, on the other hand, refers to the software embedded in various hardware components, such as the graphics card, network adapter, or storage devices. Both BIOS and firmware updates provide bug fixes, performance improvements, new features, and security patches.

Updating the BIOS and firmware can address compatibility issues, enhance system performance, and provide protection against security vulnerabilities. Manufacturers often release updates to address specific hardware or software conflicts, improve stability, and ensure optimal functioning of the system.

Before performing a BIOS or firmware update, it is essential to take certain precautions. Ensure that your system is connected to a reliable power source to prevent interruptions during the update process. Create a backup of important data to safeguard against potential data loss or system instability in case of any issues during the update.

To update the BIOS or firmware, visit the manufacturer's website and locate the support or downloads section. Identify the specific model and version of your hardware component to download the appropriate update. Carefully read the instructions provided by the manufacturer to ensure a successful update.

Updating the BIOS typically involves creating a bootable USB drive or using a manufacturer-provided utility. Follow the manufacturer's instructions to enter the BIOS setup and initiate the update process. Avoid interrupting the update or powering off the system during this process, as it can lead to irreversible damage.

Updating firmware usually requires downloading the update file from the manufacturer's website and running a utility or installer. Some components may offer automatic firmware updates through software utilities installed on your system. Follow the provided instructions carefully and avoid any disruptions during the update process.

After completing the update, restart your system and enter the BIOS setup to verify the updated version. Check the firmware versions of other hardware components as well. Ensure that the system is functioning correctly and perform any necessary configurations or optimizations based on the updated firmware.

Chapter 4: Computer Peripherals and Input Devices

Keyboard and Mouse Repair

The keyboard and mouse are essential input devices for interacting with a computer. When these peripherals encounter issues, it can significantly impact productivity and usability. In this section, we will explore common problems associated with keyboards and mice and provide effective solutions for repairing them.

Non-Responsive Keyboard or Mouse: If your keyboard or mouse is not responding, the first step is to check the physical connection. Ensure that the cables are securely plugged into the appropriate ports on your computer. For wireless devices, ensure that the batteries are charged and the devices are properly paired with the computer. If the issue persists, try connecting the keyboard or mouse to another computer to determine if it is a hardware or software problem.

Sticky or Unresponsive Keys: Sticky or unresponsive keys on a keyboard can hinder typing speed and accuracy. To address this issue, start by cleaning the keyboard. Gently remove any debris or dust particles by using compressed air or a soft brush. If specific keys are still unresponsive, carefully remove and clean them individually using a keyboard keycap puller or a small tool. Clean the keycap and the area underneath it, ensuring there is no obstruction. If cleaning does not resolve the issue, consider replacing the faulty keys or the entire keyboard if necessary.

Erratic Cursor Movement: An erratic or jumpy cursor movement can make using the mouse frustrating. Begin by cleaning the mouse's sensor, as dust or dirt accumulation can interfere with its tracking. Use a soft, lint-free cloth or a cotton swab lightly dampened with isopropyl alcohol to clean the sensor. Ensure that the mousepad or the surface you are using the mouse on is clean and free of any obstructions. If the problem persists, try using the mouse on a different surface or try a different mouse to determine if it is a hardware or software issue.

Unstable Wireless Connection: For wireless keyboards and mice, connectivity issues can arise due to interference or weak signals. Ensure that there are no obstructions between the keyboard/mouse and the wireless receiver. Keep them within a reasonable range to maintain a stable connection. If other wireless devices are present nearby, such as routers or cordless phones, they might interfere with the signal. Try changing the batteries in the keyboard or mouse, as weak batteries can cause connectivity problems.

Modifier Key Malfunctions: Modifier keys, such as Shift, Ctrl, or Alt, are vital for executing shortcuts and performing various functions. If these keys are not functioning correctly, it can impact your productivity. Firstly, check if the keys are physically stuck or damaged, and clean them if necessary. Next, verify the keyboard settings in your operating system to ensure that the modifier keys are configured correctly. If the issue persists, consider using software utilities or third-party applications to remap or redefine the modifier keys.

Monitor and Display Troubleshooting

The monitor is an integral part of any computer setup, providing visual output and allowing users to interact with their systems. However, issues with the monitor or display can be frustrating and hinder productivity. In this section, we will discuss common problems that can occur with monitors and displays and provide troubleshooting steps to resolve them effectively.

No Display or Blank Screen: If your monitor is not displaying anything or showing a blank screen, start by checking the power connection and ensure that the monitor is turned on. If the power indicator light is not lit, check the power cable and connections. If the monitor is receiving power but still not displaying anything, try connecting it to a different power outlet or testing it on another computer. If the issue persists, it may indicate a hardware problem, and professional assistance may be required.

Flickering or Distorted Display: A flickering or distorted display can strain your eyes and make it difficult to work. Begin by checking the video cable connections between the monitor and the computer. Ensure that the cables are securely connected and not damaged. If the issue persists, try connecting the monitor to a different computer or use a different video cable to determine if it is a hardware or software problem. Adjust the monitor's refresh rate and resolution settings to see if it improves the display quality.

Stuck or Dead Pixels: Stuck or dead pixels are often noticeable as small dots or discolored areas on the screen. To address this issue, try using software-based pixel fixing tools that rapidly cycle through colors to stimulate the stuck or dead pixels. You can also try gently massaging the affected area with a soft cloth or applying light pressure with a pixel fixing tool. However, exercise caution to avoid causing further damage to the monitor. If the problem persists, contact the manufacturer for further assistance or inquire about warranty coverage.

Incorrect Display Orientation: Sometimes, the display orientation may be set incorrectly, resulting in an upside-down or sideways screen. To resolve this, right-click on the desktop and access the display settings. Look for the display orientation or screen rotation settings and adjust them accordingly. Apply the changes and check if the display orientation is now correct.

Color Calibration and Display Settings: If the colors on your monitor appear distorted or inaccurate, you may need to calibrate the display. Access the display settings or use calibration tools provided by your operating system to adjust the color temperature, contrast, and gamma settings. Follow the on-screen instructions to ensure accurate color representation on your monitor.

Printer and Scanner Maintenance

Printers and scanners are essential devices for many computer users, enabling them to create physical copies of documents or digitize physical content. However, these devices require regular maintenance to ensure optimal performance and longevity. In this section, we will discuss common maintenance tasks and troubleshooting techniques for printers and scanners.

Cleaning Print Heads and Scanner Glass: Over time, print heads can become clogged or accumulate ink residue, leading to poor print quality. Similarly, scanner glass may gather dust or smudges, resulting in distorted or unclear scans. To address these issues, refer to the printer or scanner manufacturer's instructions for guidance on cleaning the print heads and scanner glass. Typically, this involves using lint-free cloths, alcohol wipes, or specialized cleaning solutions. Regular cleaning helps maintain clear prints and accurate scans.

Paper Jam Prevention and Removal: Paper jams are a common problem with printers, causing frustration and interrupting workflow. To prevent paper jams, ensure that the paper is properly aligned and not overloaded in the tray. Use the correct paper size and type recommended by the printer manufacturer. If a paper jam does occur, follow the printer's instructions for safely removing the jammed paper. Avoid using excessive force or pulling the paper forcefully, as this may damage the printer. Regularly inspect and clean the paper path to remove any debris or obstructions that may cause future jams.

Ink and Toner Cartridge Replacement: When the printer's ink or toner cartridges are running low, it can affect print quality or lead to faded prints. Refer to the printer manufacturer's instructions for the proper procedure to replace ink or toner cartridges. Take care to remove the protective packaging and install the cartridges correctly. Ensure that you use genuine cartridges or compatible ones recommended by the manufacturer to maintain optimal print quality and avoid potential damage to the printer.

Software and Driver Updates: Printer and scanner functionality can be enhanced and issues can be resolved through software and driver updates. Check the manufacturer's website for the latest drivers and software updates specific to your printer or scanner model. Install these updates to ensure compatibility with your operating system and to take advantage of new features and bug fixes. Regular updates help maintain device compatibility and performance.

Troubleshooting Common Printing and Scanning Issues: Printers and scanners may encounter various issues, such as connectivity problems, print quality issues, or scanner recognition errors. Refer to the device's user manual or online support resources provided by the manufacturer for troubleshooting steps tailored to your specific model. These resources often include step-by-step instructions for resolving common problems, performing diagnostic tests, and adjusting settings to optimize performance.

Audio Devices and Speaker Repair

Audio devices and speakers are essential components of a computer setup, allowing users to enjoy multimedia content, communicate through voice calls, and listen to music. However, issues with audio devices and speakers can arise, impacting the overall audio experience. In this section, we will explore common maintenance tasks and troubleshooting techniques for audio devices and speaker repair.

Checking Connections and Cables: Start by checking the connections and cables of your audio devices and speakers. Ensure that they are securely plugged into the correct ports on your computer or audio system. Verify that the cables are not damaged or frayed. Sometimes, loose or faulty connections can cause audio issues, so reseating the cables or replacing them may resolve the problem.

Adjusting Volume and Audio Settings: If you are experiencing low or no sound from your speakers, check the volume settings on your computer or audio device. Ensure that the volume is not muted or set to a very low level. Additionally, check the audio settings in your operating system or audio control panel to make sure the correct audio output device is selected and the settings are configured properly.

Updating Audio Drivers: Outdated or faulty audio drivers can lead to audio problems. Visit the manufacturer's website or the support page of your computer to download and install the latest audio drivers for your specific model. Updating the drivers can often resolve compatibility issues and improve audio performance.

Cleaning Speaker Components: Over time, dust and debris can accumulate on the speaker components, affecting sound quality. Gently clean the speaker grills, cones, and other components using a soft cloth or a brush. Be careful not to use excessive force or liquid that could damage the speakers. Regular cleaning helps maintain clear and crisp audio output.

Troubleshooting Audio Issues: If you are experiencing audio problems such as distorted sound, static, or audio cutting in and out, there are several troubleshooting steps you can follow. Restart your computer or audio device to rule out temporary software glitches. Test the speakers with different audio sources or devices to determine if the issue is specific to a particular source. Additionally, check the audio settings and adjust the equalizer settings to optimize sound quality.

Speaker Replacement and Repair: In some cases, speakers may need to be replaced or repaired. If you suspect a hardware issue with the speakers, consult the manufacturer's documentation or contact their support for guidance on repair options or replacement parts. Consider professional repair services if you are not confident in performing speaker repairs yourself.

Chapter 5: Storage Devices and Data Recovery

Hard Disk Drive (HDD) Maintenance

Hard Disk Drives (HDDs) are commonly used storage devices in computers, storing operating systems, applications, and personal data. To ensure the reliability and longevity of your HDD, regular maintenance is crucial. In this section, we will explore essential maintenance tasks and practices for HDDs.

Over time, your HDD may accumulate unnecessary files, temporary data, and unused applications. Performing regular disk cleanup helps optimize storage space and improve system performance. Use the built-in disk cleanup utility in your operating system or third-party software to remove temporary files, clear browser caches, and delete unnecessary files. Additionally, organize your data by creating folders and properly labeling files to improve accessibility and facilitate efficient file management.

As data is written and deleted from your HDD, it can become fragmented, leading to slower read and write speeds. Running periodic disk defragmentation helps optimize data placement on the HDD, reducing access times and improving overall performance. Your operating system may have a built-in defragmentation tool, or you can use third-party defragmentation software. Follow the instructions provided by the tool to analyze and defragment your HDD.

Monitoring the health and performance of your HDD is essential for early detection of potential issues. Utilize HDD monitoring software that provides SMART (Self-Monitoring, Analysis, and Reporting Technology) data to track parameters such as temperature, bad sectors, and overall health status. Regularly review the SMART data to identify any signs of deteriorating health or impending failure. If any abnormalities are detected, it is advisable to backup your data and consider replacing the HDD.

Proper power management is crucial for the longevity of your HDD. Avoid sudden power interruptions or fluctuations by using a reliable power supply and utilizing surge protectors or uninterruptible power supplies (UPS). Sudden power loss or voltage spikes can lead to data corruption and damage the HDD. Additionally, configure your operating system to allow the HDD to enter an idle or sleep mode after a specified period of inactivity. This helps conserve power and reduces unnecessary wear on the HDD.

When handling HDDs, it is important to follow proper precautions. Avoid dropping or subjecting the HDD to physical shocks, as this can damage the internal components and lead to data loss. Additionally, be mindful of the operating temperature and humidity levels. Extreme temperatures and high humidity can affect the performance and reliability of the HDD. Ensure that the HDD is installed in a properly ventilated area and maintain suitable environmental conditions.

Solid-State Drive (SSD) Maintenance

Solid-State Drives (SSDs) have become popular storage devices due to their speed, reliability, and durability. While SSDs require less maintenance compared to traditional hard disk drives (HDDs), there are still important maintenance tasks to ensure optimal performance and longevity. In this section, we will explore key maintenance practices for SSDs.

SSD manufacturers often release firmware updates that can improve performance, stability, and compatibility. Check the manufacturer's website or support page periodically to see if any firmware updates are available for your SSD model. Follow the instructions provided by the manufacturer to safely update the firmware. Keeping the firmware up to date can address known issues and unlock new features for your SSD.

Like HDDs, SSDs can accumulate unnecessary files and data over time. Performing regular disk cleanup helps free up space and optimize performance. Use the built-in disk cleanup utility in your operating system or third-party software to remove temporary files, clear caches, and delete unnecessary data. Additionally, SSDs support a technology called TRIM, which helps maintain performance by erasing unused data blocks. Ensure that TRIM is enabled in your operating system settings to allow the SSD to efficiently manage its storage space.

When setting up partitions on your SSD, it is important to ensure proper alignment. Misaligned partitions can lead to reduced performance and increased wear on the SSD. Most modern operating systems automatically align partitions correctly. However, if you are using an older operating system or manually creating partitions, ensure that they are aligned to the optimal boundaries recommended by the SSD manufacturer. Proper alignment ensures that data is written and read efficiently, improving overall performance.

While SSDs are reliable, it is still important to regularly back up your data. Unexpected failures or accidents can result in data loss. Implement a backup strategy that suits your needs, whether it's using an external storage device, cloud storage services, or a combination of both. Regularly schedule backups to ensure that your important files and data are protected in case of unforeseen events.

Similar to HDDs, proper power management is important for SSDs. Use a reliable power supply and consider using surge protectors or uninterruptible power supplies (UPS) to protect your SSD from sudden power interruptions or voltage fluctuations. Sudden power loss can potentially cause data corruption or loss. Additionally, configure your operating system to enable power-saving features such as sleep mode or hibernation to conserve power when the SSD is idle.

Data Backup and Recovery Methods

Data backup and recovery are critical aspects of computer hardware maintenance. Accidental file deletion, hardware failures, or malware attacks can result in data loss. Therefore, it is essential to have robust backup and recovery strategies in place. In this section, we will explore different data backup and recovery methods to safeguard your valuable information.

Regular Data Backup: Regularly backing up your data is the first line of defense against data loss. Consider creating multiple copies of your important files and storing them in different locations. You can choose from various backup methods, such as:

External Storage: Use external hard drives, USB flash drives, or network-attached storage (NAS) devices to create backups. Manually copy your files or utilize backup software to automate the process.

Cloud Storage: Cloud storage services offer convenient and secure options for backing up your data. Select a reliable cloud provider and upload your files to their servers. Ensure your data is encrypted and consider utilizing services that offer versioning and file recovery options.

Disk Imaging: Disk imaging involves creating a complete copy (image) of your entire hard drive or specific partitions. This method allows you to restore your system to a previous state, including the operating system, applications, and data.

Incremental and Differential Backups: To optimize backup storage space and reduce backup time, consider using incremental or differential backup methods. Incremental backups only store changes made since the last backup, while differential backups store changes made since the last full backup. By performing regular incremental or differential backups, you can save time and resources while ensuring that your data is up to date.

Disaster Recovery Planning: Developing a comprehensive disaster recovery plan is crucial for mitigating the impact of hardware failures, natural disasters, or other catastrophic events. Identify critical systems and data, establish recovery time objectives (RTOs) and recovery point objectives (RPOs), and create a step-by-step plan outlining the necessary actions during a crisis. Test and update your disaster recovery plan periodically to ensure its effectiveness.

Data Recovery Tools: In the unfortunate event of data loss, data recovery tools can help retrieve deleted or inaccessible files. There are numerous software applications available that specialize in data recovery. These tools scan your storage devices and attempt to recover lost data. However, note that the success of data recovery largely depends on the nature of the data loss and the condition of the storage device.

Verification and Testing: It is important to periodically verify the integrity of your backups and test the recovery process. Verify that your backups are complete and error-free, and ensure that you can successfully restore files from your backup storage. Regularly perform test recoveries to validate the effectiveness of your backup and recovery procedures.

Chapter 6: Network and Connectivity Troubleshooting

Wired and Wireless Networking Issues

In today's interconnected world, a stable and reliable network connection is essential. Wired and wireless networks can encounter various issues that can disrupt connectivity and impact productivity. In this section, we will explore common problems encountered in wired and wireless networks and discuss troubleshooting techniques to resolve them.

Connectivity Loss: One of the most common issues in network troubleshooting is the loss of connectivity. This can occur in both wired and wireless networks. Start by checking the physical connections of cables and ensure they are securely plugged in. In the case of wireless networks, verify that your device is within range of the access point and that Wi-Fi is enabled. If connectivity issues persist, try power cycling the network devices, such as routers or switches, to reset their configurations.

Slow Network Speed: Slow network speeds can significantly impact your browsing experience or the performance of network-dependent tasks. Begin troubleshooting by checking for bandwidth-intensive applications or downloads running in the background that may be consuming network resources. Ensure that your network devices, such as routers or modems, are capable of handling the speed you are subscribed to from your internet service provider (ISP). Consider performing a speed test to measure your actual network speed and compare it to the expected speed.

IP Address Conflict: IP address conflicts can occur when multiple devices on the network are assigned the same IP address, resulting in connectivity problems. To resolve this, try restarting your device, which will trigger a request for a new IP address from the network. Alternatively, you can manually release and renew the IP address from the network settings of your device. In more complex network environments, you may need to check your DHCP server settings and ensure they are properly configured to assign unique IP addresses to devices.

DNS Resolution Issues: Domain Name System (DNS) is responsible for translating domain names into IP addresses. If you are experiencing difficulty accessing websites or receiving DNS-related errors, it may indicate DNS resolution issues. To troubleshoot, try using alternative DNS servers such as Google DNS or OpenDNS. Clearing your DNS cache or flushing the DNS resolver cache on your device can also help resolve DNS-related problems.

Interference and Signal Strength: Wireless networks are susceptible to interference from neighboring Wi-Fi networks, household appliances, or physical obstructions. Poor signal strength can result in weak or unstable connections. To address this, reposition your wireless router or access point to optimize signal coverage. Avoid placing them near electronic devices that may cause interference. Consider using Wi-Fi signal boosters or range extenders to improve coverage in larger areas or multiple floors.

Security and Authentication Issues: Network security is crucial to protect your data and ensure authorized access to your network. If you are experiencing authentication or security-related problems, double-check your network security settings, including Wi-Fi passwords or encryption methods. Ensure that your devices have up-to-date antivirus software and firewalls enabled to prevent unauthorized access or malware infections.

Troubleshooting Network Interface Cards (NICs)

Network Interface Cards (NICs) play a vital role in establishing network connectivity for computers. When NICs encounter issues, it can result in network disruptions and connectivity problems. In this section, we will discuss common problems related to NICs and explore troubleshooting techniques to resolve them.

Device Recognition Issues: If your computer fails to recognize the NIC or displays error messages indicating a problem with the device, start by checking the physical connection. Ensure that the NIC is properly seated in the expansion slot and that the necessary power and data cables are securely connected. If the NIC is integrated into the motherboard, verify that it is enabled in the system BIOS settings.

Driver Problems: Outdated or incompatible NIC drivers can cause connectivity issues. Begin troubleshooting by checking for driver updates. Visit the manufacturer's website or use driver update software to download and install the latest drivers for your specific NIC model. Updating the drivers can resolve compatibility issues and improve the overall performance of the NIC.

Connectivity and Speed Problems: If you are experiencing intermittent connectivity or slow network speeds, it may be related to the NIC settings or configuration. Start by checking the network settings on your computer. Ensure that the NIC is set to obtain an IP address automatically via DHCP, unless you have specific network requirements. Check the link speed and duplex settings and ensure they match the capabilities of your network infrastructure.

Hardware Failures: In some cases, hardware failures can occur with NICs. This can be due to physical damage, component malfunction, or age-related issues. If you suspect a hardware problem, try installing the NIC in another computer or replacing it with a known working NIC to determine if the issue lies with the card itself. Additionally, inspect the NIC for any visible signs of damage or loose connections.

Resource Conflicts: NICs can sometimes conflict with other devices or components in the system, resulting in connectivity problems. Check the device manager or system logs for any indications of resource conflicts, such as IRQ or I/O address conflicts. If conflicts are detected, you may need to manually reassign resources or adjust settings to resolve the conflict.

Advanced Troubleshooting: If basic troubleshooting steps do not resolve the issue, advanced techniques may be necessary. These can include resetting the NIC configuration, performing a clean boot to isolate potential software conflicts, or using diagnostic tools provided by the NIC manufacturer. Consult the manufacturer's documentation or support resources for specific instructions on advanced troubleshooting steps.

Router and Switch Problems

Routers and switches are essential network devices responsible for directing network traffic and ensuring proper connectivity. When issues arise with routers and switches, it can lead to network disruptions and connectivity problems. In this section, we will discuss common problems related to routers and switches and explore troubleshooting techniques to address them.

Power and Connectivity Issues: Start troubleshooting router and switch problems by checking their power supply and physical connections. Ensure that the devices are receiving power and that the power cables are securely connected. Verify that network cables are properly connected to the appropriate ports and that they are not damaged or loose. If possible, try connecting a different device to the same port to determine if the issue lies with the router or switch itself.

Firmware and Configuration: Outdated firmware or misconfigured settings can cause issues with routers and switches. Begin troubleshooting by checking for firmware updates provided by the manufacturer. Update the firmware to the latest version to ensure compatibility and address known issues. Additionally, review the device's configuration settings, such as IP addresses, subnet masks, and gateway settings, to ensure they are correctly set for your network environment.

Network Addressing and DHCP Problems: Incorrect network addressing or DHCP (Dynamic Host Configuration Protocol) configuration can result in connectivity problems. Verify that the router or switch is properly configured to provide IP addresses to connected devices via DHCP. Ensure that the DHCP pool has sufficient available addresses to accommodate all connected devices. If static IP addresses are being used, double-check that they are assigned correctly and do not conflict with other devices on the network.

VLAN and Port Configuration: Virtual LANs (VLANs) and port configurations are crucial for managing network traffic and ensuring proper communication between devices. If you are experiencing connectivity issues or isolated network segments, review the VLAN and port settings on your router or switch. Ensure that the appropriate VLANs are configured and that ports are correctly assigned to the desired VLANs. Check for any VLAN mismatch or incorrect port configurations that may be causing the problem.

Spanning Tree Protocol (STP) Issues: Spanning Tree Protocol is used to prevent network loops and ensure redundant network paths operate efficiently. However, misconfigured or malfunctioning STP settings can result in network instability or connectivity problems. Verify that the STP settings on your router or switch are properly configured. Check for any STP-related error messages or events in the device logs that may indicate a problem.

Hardware Failures: Like any electronic device, routers and switches can experience hardware failures over time. This can include issues with power supplies, faulty ports, or component malfunctions. If you suspect a hardware problem, try connecting a different device to the same network port or using a different network cable to isolate the issue. Consider contacting the manufacturer's support or consulting with a professional if hardware failures are suspected.

Internet Connectivity Troubleshooting

Internet connectivity issues can be frustrating, but understanding how to troubleshoot them can help you get back online quickly. In this section, we will explore common problems related to internet connectivity and provide troubleshooting techniques to resolve them.

Check Physical Connections: Begin troubleshooting by checking the physical connections between your modem, router, and computer. Ensure that all cables are securely plugged in and that there are no visible signs of damage. If you're using a wired connection, make sure the Ethernet cable is properly connected to both the modem and the router. If you're using a wireless connection, ensure that your device is within range of the router and that there are no obstacles blocking the signal.

Restart Modem and Router: Sometimes, internet connectivity issues can be resolved by simply restarting the modem and router. Turn off both devices, wait for a few seconds, and then turn them back on. This process can help refresh the connection and resolve temporary glitches.

Verify Internet Service Provider (ISP) Status: If you're experiencing widespread internet connectivity issues, it's possible that the problem lies with your internet service provider. Check the status of your ISP by visiting their website or contacting their customer support. They may be able to provide information about any known outages or maintenance in your area.

Reset Network Settings: Incorrect network settings can also cause internet connectivity problems. Resetting your network settings can help resolve these issues. On your computer or mobile device, navigate to the network settings and look for an option to reset network settings or to forget and reconnect to the network. Follow the prompts to reset the network settings and try connecting to the internet again.

Check DNS Settings: DNS (Domain Name System) translates domain names into IP addresses and plays a crucial role in internet connectivity. Incorrect DNS settings can cause connection problems. Ensure that your device is set to obtain DNS automatically from your ISP or use reliable public DNS servers such as Google DNS (8.8.8.8 and 8.8.4.4) or Cloudflare DNS (1.1.1.1 and 1.0.0.1).

Scan for Malware: Malware infections can sometimes disrupt internet connectivity. Run a full system scan using reliable antivirus or anti-malware software to detect and remove any malicious programs that may be affecting your internet connection.

Update Firmware: Outdated firmware in your modem or router can lead to compatibility issues and connectivity problems. Visit the manufacturer's website and check for firmware updates for your specific device model. Follow the instructions provided by the manufacturer to update the firmware.

Contact ISP Support: If the above troubleshooting steps do not resolve the issue, it's advisable to contact your internet service provider's technical support. They can perform remote diagnostics, analyze your connection, and provide further assistance in resolving the problem.

Chapter 7: Upgrading and Installing Hardware Components

Understanding Compatibility and System Requirements

Before upgrading or installing hardware components in your computer, it's crucial to understand compatibility and system requirements to ensure a successful and smooth installation process. In this section, we will explore the importance of compatibility and system requirements and provide guidelines for making informed decisions.

Each hardware component, such as the CPU, RAM, motherboard, and graphics card, has specific compatibility requirements. These requirements include factors like form factor, socket type, power requirements, and supported technologies. When upgrading or installing new hardware, ensure that it is compatible with your existing components and meets the specifications outlined by the manufacturer. Check compatibility lists, consult the manufacturer's documentation, or use online resources to verify compatibility before making a purchase.

Hardware components may have specific compatibility requirements with the operating system you are using. Certain features or functionalities may not be supported by older operating systems, so it's essential to check if the hardware you plan to install is compatible with your operating system version. Verify if drivers or software updates are available for your operating system to ensure seamless integration and optimal performance.

Upgrading or installing new hardware components may require additional power. It's important to consider the power supply unit (PSU) capacity and connectors to meet the power demands of the new components. Check the power requirements of the components you plan to install and compare them to the available power output of your PSU. If necessary, upgrade your PSU to provide adequate power and ensure stable operation.

Hardware components come in various form factors, sizes, and physical designs. Before installation, assess the physical space available within your computer case to ensure the new component will fit properly. Consider factors such as the length and height of graphics cards, the size of CPU coolers, and the dimensions of storage drives. Additionally, check if the motherboard supports the form factor of the components you plan to install, such as ATX, microATX, or mini-ITX.

Upgrading hardware components can have resource implications. For example, installing additional RAM may require checking if your motherboard supports the desired capacity and type of RAM modules. Upgrading to a higher-performing CPU or GPU may require ensuring sufficient cooling solutions to dissipate heat effectively. It's important to review the system requirements of the components you plan to install and consider any necessary adjustments to optimize system performance and stability.

Some hardware upgrades may require installing specific software or drivers to fully utilize their features and functionalities. Before installation, check if the manufacturer provides the necessary software or drivers for your operating system. Ensure that you download the latest versions from reputable sources to avoid compatibility issues and maximize the capabilities of your hardware.

Installing RAM and Storage Devices

Upgrading or installing RAM and storage devices can greatly enhance your computer's performance and storage capacity. In this section, we will guide you through the process of installing RAM and storage devices, ensuring a smooth and successful installation.

Before starting the installation process, gather the necessary tools, including a screwdriver, an antistatic wrist strap (optional but recommended), and the new RAM or storage device you plan to install. Power off your computer and unplug it from the power source to ensure safety.

Installing RAM:

- Locate the RAM slots on your motherboard. Most motherboards have multiple slots for RAM, usually near the CPU socket.
- If you are replacing existing RAM, press the tabs on either side of the RAM module to release it. Gently remove the module from the slot.
- Align the notch on the new RAM module with the slot on the motherboard. Make sure the module is facing the right way.
- Firmly press down on the module until it clicks into place. The tabs on the sides should automatically lock into position, securing the RAM.
- Repeat the process if you have multiple RAM modules to install. It's important to

follow the motherboard's manual or documentation for proper installation and to ensure you're using the correct slots for optimal performance.

Installing Storage Devices:

- Identify an available drive bay in your computer case. Drive bays are typically located near the front of the case and may be labeled or color-coded.
- For a hard disk drive (HDD) or solid-state drive (SSD):

If the drive requires an adapter or bracket, attach it to the drive first.
Slide the drive into the drive bay, aligning the screw holes on the sides of the drive with those on the bay.
Secure the drive in place using screws or any other mounting mechanism provided by your case.

For an M.2 SSD:

- Locate the M.2 slot on your motherboard. It is usually located near the RAM slots or labeled accordingly.
- Insert the M.2 SSD into the slot at a slight angle, aligning the notches on the SSD with those on the slot.

- Gently press the SSD down and secure it with the screw or latch provided, if applicable.
- Connect the necessary cables to the newly installed storage device. SATA drives require a data cable (SATA cable) and a power cable (SATA power connector), while M.2 SSDs do not require additional cables.
- Once the device is properly installed and connected, carefully close your computer case and secure it with screws or latches.

Powering On and Verifying Installation: After installing RAM or storage devices, reattach the power cable, peripherals, and monitor to your computer. Power it on and check the BIOS or operating system to ensure that the newly installed components are detected and recognized. If necessary, update drivers or configure the BIOS settings to optimize performance.

Graphics Card Upgrades

Upgrading your graphics card can significantly improve your computer's visual performance and enable you to run more demanding applications and games. In this section, we will walk you through the process of upgrading your graphics card, ensuring a successful installation and optimal performance.

Compatibility Check: Before purchasing a new graphics card, it's crucial to ensure compatibility with your computer's hardware and power supply. Check the specifications of your motherboard, including the available PCIe slot type and the power supply's wattage and connectors. Ensure that the new graphics card is compatible with these requirements to avoid any compatibility issues.

Preparing for Installation:

- Power off your computer and unplug it from the power source.
- Open your computer case by removing the side panel. Consult your computer's manual if you're unsure how to do this.
- Locate the existing graphics card, usually inserted into a PCIe slot on the motherboard.
- Remove any screws or clips securing the graphics card to the case, if applicable.
- Gently disconnect the power connectors and any other cables connected to the graphics card.

Removing the Existing Graphics Card:

- Release the retention mechanism on the PCIe slot by pushing the latch or tab, depending on the design.
- Hold the graphics card firmly by its edges and gently rock it back and forth to loosen it from the slot.
- Once loosened, carefully lift the graphics card straight up to remove it from the slot.

Installing the New Graphics Card:

- Align the new graphics card with the vacant PCIe slot, ensuring that it lines up with the slot's connector.
- Gently insert the graphics card into the slot, applying equal pressure to both ends until it is fully seated.
- Secure the graphics card to the case using screws or clips, if necessary.
- Connect the necessary power cables to the graphics card. Most modern graphics cards require additional power connectors, typically PCIe power connectors.
- Double-check that all connections are secure and that the graphics card is properly seated in the slot.

Powering On and Driver Installation:

- Close your computer case and secure it with screws or latches.

- Reconnect the power cable, peripherals, and monitor.
- Power on your computer and log into your operating system.
- Download the latest drivers for your new graphics card from the manufacturer's website.
- Follow the installation instructions provided by the manufacturer to install the drivers.

Testing and Optimization:

- Once the drivers are installed, restart your computer to apply any necessary changes.
- Run benchmark tests or graphic-intensive applications to verify the performance of your new graphics card.
- Adjust the graphics settings in games or applications to optimize the visual experience according to your preferences.
- Monitor the temperatures of your graphics card using software tools to ensure it stays within safe operating limits.
- Regularly update your graphics card drivers to benefit from performance improvements and bug fixes.

CPU and Cooling System Upgrades

Upgrading your CPU and cooling system can significantly enhance your computer's processing power and improve its overall performance. In this section, we will guide you through the process of upgrading your CPU and cooling system, ensuring a smooth installation and efficient cooling for your computer.

Before upgrading your CPU, ensure that it is compatible with your motherboard's socket type. Consult your motherboard's documentation or manufacturer's website to verify compatibility. Additionally, check the power requirements of the new CPU to ensure that your power supply can handle the increased power demands.

Preparing for Installation:

- Power off your computer and disconnect it from the power source.
- Open your computer case by removing the side panel.
- Locate the existing CPU and cooling system. If a CPU cooler is already installed, you will need to remove it.

Removing the Existing CPU and Cooling System:

- Gently release the CPU socket lever to unlock the CPU.
- Lift the CPU straight out of the socket, taking care not to bend any of the pins.
- If a CPU cooler is present, detach any screws or clips securing it to the motherboard and carefully remove it.

Installing the New CPU:

- Align the new CPU with the socket, ensuring that the pins or contacts align correctly.
- Place the CPU gently into the socket, making sure it sits flat and aligns with the socket notches or markings.
- Once in place, lower the CPU socket lever to lock the CPU into position.

Upgrading the Cooling System:

- Clean the surface of the CPU and apply a thin layer of thermal paste.
- If you're using an aftermarket CPU cooler, follow the manufacturer's instructions for installation. This usually involves attaching brackets to the motherboard and securing the cooler on top of the CPU.
- Ensure that the cooler is properly secured and connected to the CPU fan header on the motherboard.

Powering On and Testing:

- Close your computer case and secure it with screws or latches.
- Reconnect the power cable and any other disconnected peripherals.
- Power on your computer and enter the BIOS/UEFI settings by pressing the designated key during startup (often Del or F2).
- Verify that the CPU is recognized correctly in the BIOS/UEFI settings and adjust any necessary settings, such as enabling XMP for memory overclocking.
- Save the changes and exit the BIOS/UEFI settings.
- Monitor your CPU temperatures using software tools and ensure they stay within acceptable ranges.

System Optimization:

- Install the latest drivers for your new CPU from the manufacturer's website.
- Run benchmark tests or CPU-intensive applications to evaluate the performance gains achieved by the CPU upgrade.
- Consider overclocking your CPU for additional performance, but proceed with caution and follow proper overclocking

guidelines to avoid damaging your hardware.

- Regularly monitor your CPU temperatures and keep an eye on system stability to ensure everything is functioning optimally.

Chapter 8: Preventive Maintenance and Cleaning

Regular Cleaning and Dust Removal

Regular cleaning and dust removal are essential for maintaining the optimal performance and longevity of your computer hardware. Over time, dust and debris can accumulate inside your computer, leading to overheating, decreased airflow, and potential hardware issues. In this section, we will guide you through the process of regular cleaning and dust removal to keep your computer running smoothly.

Before starting any cleaning procedures, ensure that your computer is powered off and unplugged from the power source. This is crucial to avoid any electrical hazards during the cleaning process.

Exterior Cleaning:

- Use a soft, lint-free cloth to gently wipe down the exterior surfaces of your computer

case, including the front panel, sides, and top.
- For stubborn stains or dirt, dampen the cloth with water or a mild cleaning solution, ensuring that the cloth is not too wet to prevent any moisture from entering the computer.
- Avoid using abrasive cleaners or sprays directly on the computer, as they may damage the finish or seep into the internal components.

Dusting the Internal Components:

- Open your computer case by removing the side panel, following the manufacturer's instructions.
- Use compressed air or a can of compressed air duster to blow away dust and debris from the internal components.
- Pay particular attention to the cooling fans, heatsinks, and the power supply unit (PSU). Hold the fans gently to prevent them from spinning while blowing out the dust.
- Ensure that you direct the airflow away from the sensitive components to avoid causing any damage.
- Use a soft brush or a small vacuum cleaner with a brush attachment to remove any remaining dust from the components.

Cleaning the Keyboard and Mouse:

- For the keyboard, turn it upside down and gently tap it to dislodge any loose debris or crumbs. You can also use compressed air to blow out the dust between the keys.
- Use a soft, slightly damp cloth or an alcohol-based wipe to clean the surfaces of the keyboard and mouse. Ensure they are completely dry before using them again.
- If you have a laptop, refer to the manufacturer's instructions on how to clean the keyboard and touchpad, as some laptops may require special care.

Display Cleaning:

- For LCD or LED monitors, use a microfiber cloth or an LCD cleaning solution to gently wipe the screen in a circular motion. Avoid using excessive pressure or spraying liquid directly on the screen.
- For CRT monitors, use a soft cloth slightly dampened with water to wipe the screen gently. Do not use any cleaning solutions or sprays on CRT screens.

Cable Management:
- Take the opportunity to organize and manage the cables inside your computer case. Use cable ties or cable management clips to bundle and secure the cables,

improving airflow and ease of maintenance in the future.

- Ensure that the cables are not blocking any cooling fans or interfering with other components.

Proper Cable Management

Proper cable management is essential for maintaining an organized and efficient computer setup. It not only improves the aesthetics of your workspace but also promotes better airflow, reduces the risk of cable damage or disconnection, and simplifies future maintenance and troubleshooting. In this section, we will explore the importance of proper cable management and provide some tips to help you achieve a tidy and well-organized cable setup.

Plan and Route Cables:

-
- Before connecting any cables, plan the layout and routing of your cables. Consider the position of your devices, the length of the cables, and the accessibility for future maintenance.

- Identify the optimal paths for each cable, avoiding areas with excessive heat, sharp edges, or heavy foot traffic.
- Group cables based on their function or destination to keep them organized. For example, separate power cables from data cables and audio cables from video cables.

Use Cable Ties and Velcro Straps:

- Secure cables together using cable ties or Velcro straps. These help prevent tangling, maintain a neat appearance, and allow for easy identification and access when needed.
- Avoid cinching the ties too tightly to prevent damage to the cables. Leave some slack to accommodate any necessary adjustments or movement.

Label Cables:

- Labeling cables can greatly simplify troubleshooting and cable management. Use cable labels or adhesive tags to identify the purpose of each cable, such as "Monitor," "Printer," or "Router."
- Alternatively, you can use color-coded cable ties or colored tape to distinguish different types of cables or connections.

Utilize Cable Management Solutions:

- Invest in cable management solutions to help route and conceal cables effectively. Cable trays, raceways, and wire channels can keep cables organized and hidden from view.
- Cable clips or adhesive cable mounts can be used to secure cables along walls, desk edges, or other surfaces, minimizing clutter and trip hazards.

Consider Cable Length:

- Use cables that are appropriate in length for your setup. Excessively long cables can create unnecessary clutter, while cables that are too short may strain connections or limit device placement.
- Coil and secure any excess cable length to prevent it from tangling or becoming a tripping hazard.

Regular Maintenance:

- Periodically check and adjust cable connections to ensure they are secure and in good condition.
- Whenever adding or removing devices or cables, take the opportunity to reassess and reorganize your cable management to maintain an orderly setup.

Cleaning Cooling Systems

Properly maintaining the cooling system of your computer is crucial for optimal performance and longevity. Over time, dust and debris can accumulate on cooling components, hindering airflow and causing the system to overheat. In this section, we will discuss the importance of cleaning cooling systems and provide guidelines on how to effectively clean them.

Understanding the Importance of Cleaning:

a. Cooling systems, such as fans and heat sinks, play a vital role in dissipating heat generated by the computer's components.
b. Dust and debris can accumulate on these components, obstructing airflow and reducing their efficiency.
c. If the cooling system is not cleaned regularly, the computer may experience overheating, which can lead to performance issues, system instability, and potential hardware damage.

Preparing for Cleaning:

- Before starting the cleaning process, ensure that the computer is turned off and disconnected from the power source.
- Gather the necessary cleaning tools, including compressed air cans or an electric air blower, lint-free cloths, and a small brush.

Cleaning the Fans:

- Locate the fans inside the computer case. These are usually found on the CPU, graphics card, and power supply unit.
- Use a can of compressed air or an electric air blower to blow away the dust and debris from the fans. Hold the fans in place to prevent them from spinning excessively.
- For stubborn dust or dirt, you can use a small brush to gently loosen and remove it.
- Be cautious not to damage any delicate fan blades or components during the cleaning process.

Cleaning Heat Sinks and Radiators:

- Heat sinks and radiators are designed to dissipate heat from components like the CPU and GPU.
- Use compressed air or an air blower to remove dust and debris from the fins of the heat sinks and radiators.

- If necessary, you can also use a brush to carefully clean between the fins.
- Avoid applying excessive force or bending the fins, as this can impair their effectiveness.

Cleaning Filters:

- Some computer cases or cooling systems may have removable dust filters. These filters help prevent dust from entering the system.
- Remove the filters and gently clean them with compressed air or by rinsing them with water and allowing them to dry completely before reinstallation.

Reassembling the System:

Once you have cleaned the cooling components, ensure that they are dry before reassembling the system.
Reconnect any disconnected cables or components and securely fasten them.
Close the computer case and ensure that all screws or latches are properly secured.

Regularly cleaning the cooling system of your computer helps maintain optimal airflow and prevents overheating. By following the guidelines provided in this section, you can effectively remove dust and debris from fans, heat sinks, and radiators, ensuring proper cooling and extending the lifespan of your computer hardware. Remember to perform routine cleaning sessions based on the specific requirements of your system and the environmental conditions in which your computer operates.

Virus and Malware Prevention

Protecting your computer from viruses and malware is essential for maintaining its security and preventing potential data loss or system damage. In this section, we will explore effective measures to prevent virus and malware infections and safeguard your computer.

Importance of Virus and Malware Prevention:

- Viruses and malware can compromise your computer's performance, steal sensitive information, and disrupt system operations.
- Prevention is key to minimizing the risk of infection and maintaining the integrity of your computer's data and software.

Implementing a Reliable Antivirus Software:

- Install a reputable antivirus software on your computer and keep it updated to defend against the latest threats.
- Configure the antivirus software to perform regular scans of your system and enable real-time protection for continuous monitoring.

Regular Operating System and Software Updates:

- Keep your operating system and software applications up to date with the latest security patches and updates.
- Many updates include essential security fixes that address vulnerabilities that malware may exploit.

Safe Internet Browsing Practices:

- Exercise caution when browsing the internet and avoid visiting suspicious or untrustworthy websites.
- Be wary of clicking on unknown or suspicious links, as they may lead to malicious websites or initiate downloads of malware.

Email Security and Phishing Awareness:

- Be cautious of email attachments and links from unknown senders, as they can contain viruses or lead to phishing attempts.
- Avoid opening attachments or clicking on links unless you are confident about their legitimacy.

Regular Data Backup:

- Backup your important files and data regularly to an external storage device or cloud-based service.
- In the event of a malware infection or system compromise, having backups ensures that you can restore your data and minimize potential losses.

User Account Privileges:

- Limit user account privileges to prevent unauthorized installations or modifications to the system.
- Use a standard user account for daily activities and reserve administrative privileges for system maintenance or software installations.

Exercise Caution with External Storage Devices:

- Scan external storage devices, such as USB drives, before accessing their contents.
- Avoid connecting unknown or suspicious devices to your computer, as they may contain malware.

Chapter 9: BIOS and Firmware Management

Understanding BIOS and UEFI

Understanding BIOS and UEFI is essential for comprehending the firmware interfaces that bridge the gap between hardware components and the operating system. In this section, we will explore the importance of BIOS and UEFI, their functionalities, and the distinctions between them.

Both BIOS and UEFI play crucial roles in a computer system by initializing hardware and facilitating the launch of the operating system. They offer vital functions such as hardware initialization, system configuration, and booting the OS.

BIOS, the traditional firmware interface, has been in use for many years. It resides in a chip on the computer's motherboard and executes during system startup. Operating through a basic input/output system, BIOS communicates with hardware components and performs low-level tasks. It typically employs the Master Boot Record (MBR) partitioning scheme.

On the other hand, UEFI is a newer firmware interface that provides several advantages over BIOS. It is stored in a firmware chip on the motherboard and offers a more advanced and feature-rich interface. UEFI supports modern capabilities such as graphical user interfaces, secure boot, and larger disk partitions using the GUID Partition Table (GPT). It boasts improved compatibility with newer hardware, faster boot times, and enhanced security features.

There are notable differences between BIOS and UEFI. Firstly, the user interface: BIOS relies on a text-based interface, while UEFI supports graphical interfaces with mouse support. Secondly, the booting process: BIOS depends on the MBR partitioning scheme and a boot loader, while UEFI uses GPT and the EFI system partition. Thirdly, disk support: BIOS is limited to 2.2TB disk sizes, while UEFI can handle larger disks. Lastly, secure boot: UEFI incorporates Secure Boot, a feature that verifies the OS's integrity and prevents the execution of unauthorized code during the boot process.

Accessing the BIOS or UEFI settings is typically achieved by using specific key combinations (e.g., F2, Del, or Esc) during the computer's startup. Within these settings, you can configure various options such as the boot order, hardware settings, and security features.

Updating BIOS and Firmware

Updating the BIOS and firmware of your computer is crucial for maintaining system stability, improving performance, and ensuring compatibility with the latest hardware and software. In this section, we will delve into the significance of updating BIOS and firmware, the update process, and precautions to consider.

Regularly updating the BIOS and firmware is important because it addresses known issues, bugs, and vulnerabilities, enhancing system stability and security. Firmware updates can also bring improvements to hardware functionality, introduce new features, and optimize performance.

To check for BIOS and firmware updates, visit the manufacturer's website for your computer or hardware component. Look for the specific model and download the latest BIOS or firmware version applicable to your system.

Before updating, it is essential to read the release notes or documentation provided with the update to understand the changes and requirements. Additionally, ensure that your computer is connected to a stable power source to prevent interruptions during the update process. Backing up your important data is also recommended to safeguard against any unforeseen issues that may arise during the update.

Updating the BIOS typically involves creating a bootable USB drive or using a built-in utility provided by the manufacturer. You will need to restart your computer and access the BIOS settings by pressing the designated key during startup. From there, navigate to the BIOS update section and select the file from the USB drive or specify the update location. Follow the on-screen instructions to initiate the update process and avoid interrupting or turning off the computer until it completes.

For firmware updates, different hardware components may require specific procedures. Download the firmware update file provided by the manufacturer and follow their instructions for installation. Some firmware updates can be installed directly within the operating system using dedicated utilities or firmware management tools.

After completing the update process, restart your computer and enter the BIOS to verify that the new version is installed. For firmware updates, you can check the device or component properties in the operating system or use manufacturer-provided tools to confirm the updated version.

When updating BIOS and firmware, it is important to take precautions and follow guidelines. Ensure that you are using the correct BIOS or firmware update for your specific hardware model and revision. Avoid interrupting the update process, as it can lead to system instability or hardware damage. If you encounter any issues during the update, consult the manufacturer's support resources or forums for troubleshooting guidance.

Troubleshooting BIOS Issues

The BIOS (Basic Input/Output System) is a critical component of your computer's hardware that initializes and controls various system functions. Occasionally, you may encounter issues with the BIOS that can affect system startup or performance. In this section, we will explore common BIOS problems and provide troubleshooting steps to resolve them.

Common BIOS Problems:

- Failure to boot or startup errors: This can be caused by incorrect BIOS settings, incompatible hardware, or corrupted BIOS data.

- Incorrect or missing BIOS settings: Inaccurate configurations can lead to issues such as system instability, boot failures, or hardware compatibility problems.
- BIOS update failures: An unsuccessful BIOS update can result in a non-functional system or cause instability.

Troubleshooting Steps:

- Ensure hardware compatibility: Verify that all installed hardware components are compatible with the BIOS version and properly seated in their respective slots.
- Reset BIOS settings: Access the BIOS and restore the default settings or use the provided option to reset the configuration to its default state.
- Update or reflash the BIOS: If experiencing issues, check for the latest BIOS version available for your motherboard or system and perform an update if necessary. Follow the manufacturer's instructions carefully to avoid any complications.
- Clear CMOS: In cases of persistent issues, resetting the CMOS (Complementary Metal-Oxide-Semiconductor) memory can help resolve configuration-related problems. Consult your motherboard manual for instructions on how to clear CMOS.
- Check hardware connections: Ensure that all cables and connectors are securely

attached to their respective ports, especially those related to storage drives or boot devices.

- Perform a hardware diagnostic: Use built-in diagnostic tools or third-party software to test hardware components for any faults or failures.
- Seek professional assistance: If troubleshooting steps do not resolve the issue or if you are uncomfortable working with the BIOS, consider contacting a computer technician or the manufacturer's support for further assistance.

Precautions:

- Be cautious when updating the BIOS: Ensure you are using the correct BIOS version for your specific motherboard model to avoid potential compatibility issues or system instability.
- Backup important data: Before performing any major BIOS changes or updates, back up critical data to safeguard against any unforeseen problems.
- Follow manufacturer's instructions: Always refer to the manufacturer's documentation and guidelines when performing BIOS troubleshooting or making changes to BIOS settings.

BIOS Recovery:

In the event of a failed BIOS update or corruption, many motherboards provide a recovery mechanism. Refer to your motherboard's manual or the manufacturer's support website for instructions on BIOS recovery procedures.

Chapter 10: Hardware Security and Protection

Protecting Against Physical Damage and Theft

Ensuring the security and protection of your computer hardware is essential in safeguarding your data and maintaining the longevity of your system. In this section, we will explore strategies and measures to protect against physical damage and theft, reducing the risk of hardware loss or compromise.

Physical Security Measures:

- Secure your workspace: Keep your computer in a locked room or secure area to restrict access and minimize the chances of unauthorized physical tampering.
- Use cable locks: Use cable locks to secure your computer and peripherals to a fixed object, such as a desk, preventing theft or unauthorized removal.
- Install security cameras: Implementing surveillance cameras in your workspace can

act as a deterrent and provide evidence in the event of theft or unauthorized access.

- Protect against power surges: Use surge protectors or uninterruptible power supply (UPS) devices to safeguard your hardware against power fluctuations and electrical surges.
- Implement physical barriers: Consider installing security bars or grilles on windows or using security alarms to deter break-ins.

Data Protection Measures:

- Regularly back up your data: Create frequent backups of your important files and store them in a secure location or on cloud-based storage services.
- Implement data encryption: Encrypt sensitive data to protect it from unauthorized access, even if the hardware is stolen or compromised.
- Use strong passwords and authentication: Set strong passwords for your computer and enable multi-factor authentication to prevent unauthorized access to your system and data.
- Enable tracking software: Install tracking software on your laptop or mobile devices to locate them in case of theft. This can help in recovery efforts and provide evidence to law enforcement.

- Educate employees or family members: Raise awareness about physical security measures and the importance of protecting hardware and data to ensure everyone understands their role in maintaining security.

Prevention and Preparedness:

- Install antivirus and security software: Protect your computer against malware and viruses by using reputable antivirus software and keeping it up to date.
- Maintain up-to-date software and firmware: Regularly update your operating system, drivers, and firmware to ensure you have the latest security patches and bug fixes.
- Secure wireless networks: Implement strong Wi-Fi passwords, enable network encryption, and change default router settings to secure your wireless network from unauthorized access.
- Restrict administrative privileges: Limit administrative access to your computer to authorized individuals to prevent unauthorized changes or installations.
- Create an inventory: Maintain a detailed inventory of your hardware, including serial numbers, purchase dates, and warranty information. This can be useful for insurance claims and recovery efforts in case of theft or damage.

Implementing Passwords and Encryption

Passwords and encryption are essential for hardware security, providing layers of protection for sensitive data. In this section, we will explore best practices for implementing strong passwords and encryption techniques to enhance the security of your computer hardware.

Creating strong passwords is crucial to protect your accounts and devices. Use complex and unique passwords that are at least 8-12 characters long and include a combination of uppercase and lowercase letters, numbers, and special characters. Avoid easily guessable information and refrain from password reuse. Enable multi-factor authentication (MFA) whenever possible to add an extra layer of security. Consider using a password manager to securely store and generate strong passwords for your various accounts.

Data encryption adds an additional level of protection to sensitive information. Implement full disk encryption (FDE) to encrypt your entire hard drive, safeguarding data even if the physical drive is lost or stolen. Use encryption tools or software to encrypt specific files or folders containing sensitive information. Enable Transport Layer Security (TLS) on network connections, especially when transmitting sensitive data over the internet. Consider using Virtual Private Networks (VPNs) for secure remote access and protection when connecting to public Wi-Fi networks.

Follow security and encryption best practices to enhance your hardware security. Keep your software up to date, including the operating system, antivirus software, and encryption tools, to ensure you have the latest security patches and features. Enable secure boot and set a password in your BIOS or UEFI firmware to protect against unauthorized modifications. Regularly change passwords, especially for critical accounts or systems. Securely store and manage encryption keys, considering hardware-based encryption solutions for added security. Educate yourself and others about password security, phishing awareness, and the risks of weak or compromised passwords.

By implementing strong passwords and encryption techniques, you can significantly enhance the security of your computer hardware and protect your sensitive data from unauthorized access. These practices form a critical part of a comprehensive security strategy and help safeguard your information in an increasingly interconnected and digital world.

Software Firewalls and Antivirus Protection

Software firewalls and antivirus programs play a vital role in protecting your computer hardware from malicious threats. In this section, we will explore the importance of these tools and provide guidelines for their effective implementation.

Software Firewalls act as a barrier between your computer and the internet, monitoring and filtering network traffic to prevent unauthorized access. It is crucial to install a reputable software firewall from a trusted vendor and keep it regularly updated to stay protected against emerging threats. Configure the firewall settings based on your security needs, allowing or blocking specific applications or services, enabling intrusion detection systems, and setting up rules to restrict network traffic. Ensure that the firewall software is regularly updated to receive the latest security patches and improvements.

Antivirus Protection is essential for detecting and eliminating malware, viruses, and other malicious software from your computer. Install a reputable antivirus program that offers real-time protection and frequent virus definition updates. Configure the antivirus software to perform scheduled scans of your system to detect and remove malware, and run on-demand scans whenever you suspect a potential infection. Keep the antivirus software updated with the latest malware signatures and detection techniques by enabling automatic virus definition updates.

In addition to software firewalls and antivirus programs, there are other security measures you should follow. Regularly update your operating system, applications, and plugins to patch security vulnerabilities and protect against known exploits. Exercise caution when downloading and opening files, ensuring they come from trusted sources. Scan downloaded files with your antivirus software before opening them. Download software and applications only from reputable sources, such as official vendor websites or reputable app stores, to minimize the risk of downloading malware-infected files. Implement a backup strategy to regularly create copies of your important files and store them securely. Backups can help restore your data in the event of a security incident or hardware failure.

By implementing software firewalls, antivirus protection, and following additional security measures, you can significantly enhance the security of your computer hardware. These tools and practices work together to safeguard your system against malicious threats, providing a strong defense for your sensitive data and ensuring the integrity and stability of your hardware.

Chapter 11: Laptop Repair and Maintenance

Common Laptop Hardware Issues

Laptops offer portability and convenience, but they can experience various hardware issues. In this section, we will explore common laptop hardware problems and provide guidance on how to identify and address them effectively.

Overheating is a significant concern for laptops. Dust accumulation in cooling vents, malfunctioning fans, or improper ventilation can cause overheating, leading to performance issues and potential component damage. Signs of overheating include sudden shutdowns, excessive fan noise, or the laptop becoming too hot to touch. To prevent overheating, regularly clean the cooling vents and fans using compressed air and ensure proper airflow by using the laptop on a flat, hard surface. Consider using a laptop cooling pad for additional ventilation.

Battery problems are another common issue. If the laptop battery is not charging properly, it could be due to a faulty power adapter, damaged charging port, or a worn-out battery. If the battery drains quickly even when not in use, it may indicate a failing battery or power-hungry background processes. Troubleshooting steps include trying a different power adapter and charging cable, and if the problem persists, consider replacing the battery or seeking professional assistance.

Screen issues can arise, such as a flickering or dim display, or a cracked or damaged screen. A loose connection between the display and the motherboard, a faulty inverter, or a failing backlight can cause screen flickering or dimness. Accidental drops or impacts can result in a cracked or broken screen. Check the display cable connections and ensure they are secure. If the issue persists, consult a professional technician for screen replacement or repair.

Keyboard and touchpad problems are common as well. Dust, debris, or liquid spills can cause sticky or unresponsive keys, while touchpad issues may arise from driver conflicts or physical damage. Cleaning the keyboard and touchpad with compressed air can remove debris, and following manufacturer guidelines for cleaning can address stubborn stains or spills. Update or reinstall touchpad drivers if necessary.

Connectivity issues, particularly with Wi-Fi and Bluetooth, can be troublesome. Difficulty connecting to Wi-Fi networks or pairing with Bluetooth devices may indicate driver issues or hardware malfunctions. Troubleshooting steps include ensuring Wi-Fi and Bluetooth are enabled, updating the drivers, and seeking assistance from the manufacturer's support or a qualified technician if the problem persists.

By understanding and addressing these common laptop hardware problems, you can keep your laptop running smoothly and prolong its lifespan. Regular maintenance, timely repairs, and seeking professional assistance when needed will help you overcome these challenges and ensure optimal performance from your laptop.

Keyboard and Trackpad Replacement

The keyboard and trackpad are crucial components of a laptop, and if they develop issues or get damaged, it can greatly affect your productivity. To replace a laptop's keyboard and trackpad, you need to first assess the problem by identifying specific issues like unresponsive keys or erratic cursor movement. It's important to ensure that the replacement keyboard or trackpad is compatible with your laptop's make and model.

To gather the necessary tools, refer to the manufacturer's instructions or online resources provided by the manufacturer. Typically, you'll need a small Phillips screwdriver, tweezers, a plastic pry tool, and an anti-static wrist strap.

Start by powering off the laptop and, if applicable, removing the battery. Follow the manufacturer's instructions to disassemble the laptop, removing any necessary panels or screws that secure the keyboard or trackpad in place. Carefully disconnect the ribbon cable or connectors that connect the keyboard or trackpad to the motherboard. Gently lift out the old keyboard or trackpad from its housing.

When installing the new keyboard or trackpad, align it correctly in the designated area and reconnect the ribbon cable or connectors to the appropriate ports on the motherboard. Replace any screws or fasteners according to the manufacturer's instructions and reassemble the laptop by putting back any panels or covers that were removed. If applicable, insert the battery into its compartment.

After the replacement, power on the laptop and plug in the power cable to check if the new keyboard or trackpad is functioning correctly. Test all the keys and trackpad functions to ensure they are responsive. If necessary, install any required driver updates from the manufacturer's website to ensure optimal performance.

It's important to follow the manufacturer's instructions and take necessary precautions during the replacement process. If you're unsure or uncomfortable performing the replacement yourself, it's recommended to seek professional assistance or contact the manufacturer's support for further guidance.

Display and Battery Maintenance

The laptop's display and battery are vital components that require proper care and maintenance for optimal performance and longevity. To maintain the laptop's display, use a soft, lint-free cloth or microfiber cloth to gently wipe the screen in a circular motion. Avoid harsh chemicals or abrasive materials that could damage the display. For stubborn smudges or fingerprints, slightly dampen the cloth with water or a screen cleaning solution designed for electronics. Consider using a screen protector to prevent scratches and smudges, ensuring it is compatible with your laptop's screen size.

When it comes to battery maintenance, avoid overcharging or fully draining the battery before recharging. It's recommended to keep the battery charge between 20% and 80% for optimal lifespan. Adjust the power management settings in your laptop's operating system to optimize battery usage. Use the "Power Saver" mode when running on battery power to conserve energy. Additionally, clean the battery contacts periodically by using a clean cloth or cotton swab dipped in rubbing alcohol to gently clean the contacts.

For battery calibration, occasionally perform a full discharge and recharge cycle to recalibrate the battery. Allow the battery to completely discharge until the laptop shuts down and then recharge it to 100%. Some laptops have built-in battery calibration tools provided by the manufacturer. Refer to the user manual or access the manufacturer's website for instructions on using these tools.

If your laptop is connected to an external display, clean the display surface using the same guidelines as for the laptop's screen. Ensure that the cables connecting your laptop to the external display are securely plugged in and check for any loose or damaged cables that may cause display issues. Use the display settings in your laptop's operating system to optimize the resolution, brightness, and color settings of the external display.

Laptop Cleaning and Cooling

Proper cleaning and cooling are essential for maintaining the performance and longevity of your laptop. To clean the external surfaces, start by shutting down the laptop and unplugging it from the power source. Use compressed air to gently blow out dust and debris from the keyboard, vents, and ports. Hold the canister upright and use short bursts to prevent liquid from spraying out. Wipe the laptop's exterior surfaces, including the keyboard, touchpad, and casing, with a soft, lint-free cloth slightly dampened with water or a mild cleaning solution. Avoid excessive moisture during this process.

For internal cleaning, consult the laptop's user manual for instructions on safely removing the bottom panel to access the internal components. Use compressed air to blow out dust and debris from the cooling fans, heat sinks, and air vents. Be thorough but gentle to avoid damaging delicate components. If necessary, remove the keyboard and touchpad to clean underneath them using a soft brush or compressed air. Wipe the surfaces with a cloth dampened with a mild cleaning solution.

To optimize the laptop's cooling system, place it on a hard, flat surface or use a cooling pad to elevate it slightly. This improves airflow and helps dissipate heat more efficiently. Install software to monitor the laptop's temperature and fan speed, allowing you to keep an eye on the system's heat levels and take appropriate action if necessary. Avoid using the laptop on soft surfaces like beds or couches, as these can obstruct airflow and cause overheating.

In terms of regular maintenance, establish a cleaning routine based on your usage and environment to prevent dust buildup and maintain optimal performance. Keep the laptop in a clean environment and avoid using it in dusty or dirty surroundings whenever possible to reduce the likelihood of debris entering the system and clogging the cooling components. If you are uncomfortable performing internal cleaning yourself, consider taking your laptop to a professional technician for thorough cleaning and maintenance.

Chapter 12: Future Trends and Emerging Technologies

Advancements in Hardware Repair and Maintenance

The field of hardware repair and maintenance is undergoing significant advancements that are shaping the future of the industry. Automated diagnostic tools and software have become more prevalent, allowing technicians to quickly analyze hardware components, detect issues, and provide detailed reports for efficient troubleshooting and repair. Additionally, remote diagnostic capabilities have gained popularity, enabling technicians to diagnose and troubleshoot hardware issues remotely, resulting in faster response times and reduced on-site visits.

Augmented Reality (AR) and Virtual Reality (VR) technologies are being integrated into hardware repair processes. AR-assisted repairs provide technicians with real-time visual guidance and information overlay, enhancing their ability to identify components, follow repair instructions, and perform intricate repairs accurately. VR training simulations offer realistic simulated environments for technicians to practice hardware repair procedures, improving skills and confidence without the need for physical hardware.

Artificial Intelligence (AI) and Machine Learning (ML) algorithms are transforming hardware repair and maintenance. Predictive maintenance utilizes AI and ML to analyze data and identify patterns, enabling proactive maintenance to replace or repair components before they cause significant issues. AI-powered systems provide intelligent repair recommendations based on previous repair data, user feedback, and expert knowledge, assisting technicians in making informed decisions and increasing repair efficiency.

Hardware manufacturers are adopting modular and upgradable designs, featuring modular components that allow for easier replacement or upgrade of specific parts without replacing the entire system. This modular approach simplifies repair and maintenance, reducing downtime and costs. User-friendly designs encourage consumers to perform their own upgrades and repairs, extending the lifespan of their hardware.

Sustainability and environmentally-friendly practices are gaining prominence in the hardware repair industry. Manufacturers are designing hardware with repairability and recyclability in mind, incorporating features like replaceable batteries and using materials that are easier to recycle, reducing electronic waste and promoting sustainability. Eco-friendly repair processes, such as using environmentally-friendly cleaning agents, reducing energy consumption during repairs, and promoting responsible disposal of electronic waste, are being adopted to minimize the environmental impact of hardware repair activities.

These recent advancements in hardware repair and maintenance reflect the industry's commitment to efficiency, user empowerment, sustainability, and staying ahead of the evolving technology landscape.

Impact of IoT and Edge Computing

The emergence of the Internet of Things (IoT) and edge computing is having a profound impact on hardware repair and maintenance practices, presenting new challenges and opportunities for professionals in the field.

IoT enables hardware devices to be interconnected and communicate with each other, allowing for real-time data on performance and health. This connectivity facilitates remote monitoring and diagnostics, empowering technicians to proactively identify and address issues before they escalate. Advanced analytics and machine learning algorithms applied to the vast amounts of data collected by IoT devices enable predictive maintenance, optimizing maintenance schedules and resource utilization.

Edge computing brings computational capabilities closer to the devices themselves, reducing reliance on centralized servers. This localized processing and analysis enable faster real-time monitoring and decision-making, even in environments with limited connectivity. Maintenance tasks can be distributed across devices and local networks, enhancing response times, reducing dependence on external infrastructure, and increasing overall system resilience.

However, the adoption of IoT and edge computing also raises security and privacy considerations. Robust security measures must be implemented to protect against unauthorized access and data breaches. Hardware repair and maintenance professionals need to be well-versed in secure protocols, encryption techniques, and authentication mechanisms. Privacy regulations and best practices should be followed to ensure the protection of sensitive user data during repair processes.

The evolving landscape of IoT and edge computing demands a broadened technical knowledge base for hardware repair professionals. In addition to traditional hardware repair skills, technicians must understand networking, cybersecurity, and data analytics. Continuous learning and upskilling will be necessary to meet the evolving demands of the industry. Collaboration between hardware technicians, software developers, and data analysts will become increasingly important in addressing the complex challenges posed by these technologies.

Scalability and infrastructure present further challenges. Large-scale IoT deployments require efficient management strategies for maintenance, updates, and scalability. Hardware repair professionals need to develop expertise in managing and maintaining these infrastructures effectively. Additionally, a reliable and resilient network infrastructure is essential for seamless edge computing operations, and technicians should be proficient in diagnosing and troubleshooting infrastructure-related issues.

In summary, the emergence of IoT and edge computing has revolutionized hardware repair and maintenance. It has enabled remote monitoring, predictive maintenance, localized processing, and distributed maintenance systems. However, it also requires heightened security and privacy measures, a broadened skillset, collaboration across disciplines, and expertise in managing large-scale deployments and infrastructure. Adapting to these changes will be key to succeeding in the future of hardware repair and maintenance.

AI-Assisted Hardware Diagnosis and Repair

The integration of artificial intelligence (AI) in hardware diagnosis and repair processes has a transformative impact on the field, revolutionizing efficiency, accuracy, and the overall customer experience.

AI algorithms bring automated diagnostics to hardware repair by analyzing performance data, identifying patterns, and detecting potential faults or anomalies. This intelligent fault detection capability enables quick identification of hardware issues, reducing manual effort and enhancing troubleshooting accuracy. Furthermore, AI systems can leverage continuous monitoring to predict potential failures, allowing for proactive maintenance and preventing costly downtime.

AI-powered systems provide guided repair and troubleshooting through step-by-step instructions and real-time feedback. Technicians can follow interactive interfaces that reduce human error and ensure effective repairs. AI systems also access vast databases of repair information, including manuals, schematics, and historical data. This wealth of knowledge enables technicians to quickly access relevant information, improving repair accuracy and efficiency.

AI technologies facilitate remote assistance and collaboration. Through augmented reality (AR) or virtual reality (VR) interfaces, experts can visually guide technicians through complex repair tasks, eliminating the need for on-site visits in some cases. AI-assisted platforms also enable collaboration among technicians and experts, allowing them to share knowledge, insights, and troubleshooting strategies for more effective problem-solving.

Ethical considerations are essential in the use of AI. AI systems should be designed and used ethically, ensuring transparency, fairness, and accountability. Proper data handling and privacy protection are crucial to maintain customer trust and ensure responsible deployment of AI-assisted hardware repair technologies. It's important to recognize that AI should complement human expertise rather than replace it. Human intuition, creativity, and critical thinking remain vital in complex repair scenarios that require a deep understanding of hardware systems.

AI algorithms have the ability to continuously learn from past repair experiences, improving diagnostic accuracy and repair recommendations over time.

This self-improvement capability enables AI systems to adapt to new hardware technologies and evolving repair challenges. Technicians in the field of hardware repair need to acquire new skills to effectively work with AI-assisted systems. Continuous learning and staying updated with the latest advancements in AI will be crucial for professionals in this domain.

AI-assisted hardware diagnosis and repair bring automated diagnostics, guided repair, remote assistance, and collaboration to the field. These technologies offer benefits such as increased efficiency, accuracy, and proactive maintenance. Ethical considerations, the complementing of human expertise, continuous learning, and technical upskilling are essential for the responsible and effective deployment of AI in hardware repair and maintenance.

Conclusion

In this comprehensive guide, we embarked on a journey to demystify the world of computer hardware repair and maintenance. From the basics of understanding computer components to troubleshooting common issues and exploring emerging technologies, we have covered a wide range of topics aimed at beginners in the field. Our goal has been to provide a smooth learning experience, empowering readers to handle hardware-related challenges with confidence.

Throughout the book, we emphasized the importance of regular hardware maintenance. We highlighted the significance of keeping computer systems in optimal condition to ensure their longevity, performance, and reliability. By following best practices and implementing preventive measures, readers can proactively address potential issues and avoid costly downtime.

We delved into the fundamental tools necessary for hardware repair, emphasizing the significance of having a well-equipped toolkit. From screwdrivers and pliers to diagnostic software and multimeters, we explored the essential tools that every aspiring technician should possess.

Safety measures and precautions were given utmost importance. We emphasized the significance of grounding techniques, proper handling of sensitive components, and protecting oneself from electrical hazards. By adhering to these safety guidelines, readers can ensure their well-being and safeguard the integrity of the hardware they work with.

Our exploration of computer components, such as the CPU, RAM, storage devices, GPU, motherboard, and power supply unit, provided readers with a solid understanding of their functionalities and maintenance requirements. We discussed common issues associated with these components and offered step-by-step instructions for repair and replacement when necessary.

In our troubleshooting chapters, we addressed various hardware-related problems, ranging from overheating and power issues to memory and display glitches. By identifying the symptoms, understanding the underlying causes, and following our troubleshooting methodologies, readers can efficiently diagnose and resolve these issues.

We also delved into the realm of peripherals and input devices, covering keyboard and mouse repair, monitor and display troubleshooting, printer and scanner maintenance, and audio device repair. By understanding these peripherals and learning how to address common problems, readers can enhance their overall computer experience.

Additionally, we explored data recovery methods, network and connectivity troubleshooting, hardware upgrades, preventive maintenance, and the importance of hardware security and protection. We discussed emerging technologies, such as IoT, edge computing, AI-assisted diagnosis, and future trends in hardware repair and maintenance.

Throughout the book, we emphasized the significance of continuous learning and staying updated with the latest advancements in the field. As technology evolves, so do the challenges and opportunities in hardware repair and maintenance. By embracing new technologies, honing their skills, and adapting to changing landscapes, readers can position themselves as competent and knowledgeable professionals in the industry.

In conclusion, this book has provided a comprehensive foundation for beginners in the field of computer hardware repair and maintenance. It has equipped readers with the knowledge, skills, and confidence needed to handle common hardware issues, perform preventive maintenance, troubleshoot problems, and embrace emerging technologies. By following the principles and techniques outlined in this book, readers can embark on a fulfilling journey in the world of computer hardware repair and maintenance, offering valuable support to individuals and organizations alike.